HUMAN WHISPERS

HUMAN WHISPERS

Samuel Appiah

authorHOUSE®

AuthorHouse™ UK
1663 Liberty Drive
Bloomington, IN 47403 USA
www.authorhouse.co.uk
Phone: 0800.197.4150

Published by AuthorHouse 11/05/2014

ISBN: 978-1-4969-9428-8 (sc)
ISBN: 978-1-4969-9429-5 (e)

DEDICATION

To all those who want to hear other people's hardships so
as to be comforted in their own

Contents

ACKNOWLEDGMENT

You help me breath, oxygen from trees. Shelter my head from rain, leaves on the trees. Keep me safe from the blazing sun, shade from trees. Keep me warm in the furiously cold winter, firewood from trees.

Provided the root cause so I could write these on this piece of ....

Thank you nature.

9 Miles Away

Cool summer's night you've gone for a ride
At night time with company by your side
Before 9 miles you encounter a bump
Tears fall after doctor told you it was more than a lump
Some arrive prematurely
An implication that can affect the baby
Whereas a few arrive in a set of two
Genealogy dependent on some that have gone for a ride
before you
9 miles later after the ride is done
There are two places a child can work with option of one
With Mr. Rod and his staff
Or Mr. Insubordinate in face of elders always laugh
The parents assist in such a decision
Evident in the way the child has been risen
9 mile ride in poor weather conditions
Can have, on one, immense implications
Poor weather can include many a thing
From a child born to parents without a wedding ring
To the dis-obedient engaged in teenage pregnancy
A trend that runs through many a family
Or is this how many a family start?

Daughter kicked out of home dis-obedience in her luggage
In a lonely state, anyone will do for homage
A son of dis-obedience offers her a lift
9 miles later everything is moving so swift
He stops the lift he offered her
Leaving her by the curb shouting he don't care
Daughter now has a baby in her baggage

No money to pay for rent or a mortgage
Hostel to live in is her best bet
Her weather condition is bad regardless how much sun shine she
may get
All because she rejected her parents umbrella
A covering in comparison to none other

Umbrella since birth is the best you can receive
Protecting from bad weather and anything else one may conceive
Covering looks over in case you implement a wrong decision
Covering protects from weather of any condition
Blazing heat in the affairs of man
A covering will teach diligence in a plan
Thus shielding from any harmful rays
Covering keeps you dry and calm on any rainy day
Whether it is physical rain or gloom of a circumstance
Umbrella keeps you sane in your walk or stance
360 degree spherical protection over you
If you think you can talk behind their back you're a fool

In God I land all my trust
For all His ways are true and just

A Nod

Acknowledge and appreciate You with a nod
You are good You are God
Comfort in the staff, discipline in the rod
In the silence of my tongue You discern my heart
My condition is evident whether I laugh or fart
You are so wonderful and marvelous
A description of you word's can't express
Your name may I be given the grace to bless
May my larynx and my tongue
Have a new way to praise better than the prior one
The thought of You causes my words to mu, mu mumble
Walking along the road Your grace permits me to stumble
I have greater things to feel embarrassment over
Laugh as they may please
They know not of You whom I praise on my knees
They may be clueless of Your splendor
Haven't seen so they automatically limit Your power
Traditions keep them trapped like a cocoon
Operating daily lives via stars signs and contour of the moon

Nothing goes right when the devil is the root of your stem
The Lord God wants none to perish
A saved, non-ignorant soul does He relish
What God has achieved
Has caused many to grieve
The work the Lord is doing
Is giving many people a blessing
The work the Lord God is doing in me I know not
I'm thankful He is doing a work and of me He has not forgot
A thank you for Your love that reaches from here to there
Which I can only express with a nod and a tear

A Rabbit

Was horny as a rabbit
Only by His grace was I able to kick the habit
Anything would do
After a quick fix then I'd be on the go
Standard temperature 37 degrees
My blood felt constantly hot above my knees
Eye's blazing hot, turning left to right
Waiting for those curves to catch my sight
There it goes again
My eyes have found a friend
Here comes my approach
My feet moving swifter than a cockroach

Hey baby what's your name?
Seen you across the way
Thought I'd come over with something to say
Can I have your number I want to give you a ding
If you're lucky one day a diamond wedding ring
What do you say let's meet next week
I'll call you tomorrow so we may speak

Walking down the street oblivious to the road
Jacket zipped up embracing the cold

There's a trap on the way but I don't know bout it
Walking down the road thinking of lyrics to spit

Who is this approaching me from across the way?
Looking kinda buff I wander if she wants to play

Is it worth it, no it is not
Eternity or the condemnation after life feeing very hot
Once sin takes over it's mindset is so what
Righteousness within exclaims hell is so hot
Right and wrong I most definitely know
But man has his own will he likes to follow
Man's will is subtle death
Corroding his brain cells till there are none left
Wisdom and knowledge are just and true
Follow these you'll be sure to get through

A Seed

A seed to be used
Like honey to a bumble bee
A sweet connection

In all the dirt from the past
God saw potential that could last
Got dug out from worldly dirt and turmoil
To be placed in the earth's purified soil
Watered with wisdom, what a sweet taste
Heat from the sun shining on my face
All ingredients for a pure seed
Wisdom readily available for many to read
God waiting to provide honesty and conviction
Multiple vessels provide the distinction

Watered by truth written in books with many a word
Meditation on what one has learned
While being watered careful of the distraction
That will please your eyes and ears with attraction
Everything you need is already in creation
Leave your worries dormant at the train station
Lack of water can cause you to shrivel
A dry season that may cause your faith to swivel
Minimal heat causes your spirit to go pale
Hiding from the light leaving your body to go stale

God don't only cut off my wasting stem
The evil root will only re grow them
God eliminate the root cause
Dig in deep loosen procrastination's claws
Be attentive to my request while I am on all fours
Lead me in direction of all Your open doors

I am dry please water my soul with Your knowledge
Feed me Your word let it be a lamp onto my feet
A seed I am uproot my non productive
Discipline of my flesh may I be conductive
Attentive to your light may I forever be
Only your water can make me grow healthy

Thank you God for accepting me as a plant
For growth in your ways my physical power can't
Absolute praise and honour is due onto Your name
All gratitude and thanks to you as I will never remain the same

Able

Add Li to able
You get liable
Add Reli to able
You get reliable
Add capa to able
You get capable

Your house being repossessed is your fault for spending idle
It is your house, no one else is to blame, you're held liable
You pray and regularly go to church so you ask why God has done
this to you
Read Mark 11:25 this might give you a clue
Forgive others so you can be forgiven and have an answer to
your prayer
That way you will never have to see another red letter
Be knowledgeable when your life is not in a bad situation
So you will be ready for any bad news or poor health condition
There is no one else humans can rely on
No other worthy of praise in deed or song
There is only one to rely on He is without fault
Reigning in Glory abolishing works of the occult
He is He who is reliable
Every work laid on firm foundation completely stable
Harvest is plentiful yet workers are few
Some apply to work not knowing what to do
Doesn't mean you remain idle
Shouldn't result in dirty mag being chosen over the Bible
Why get down with the devil when God can give you a lift
Or are you willing to give up that free gift?
Devil wont discriminate on who he will rape
Come to steal your word sweeter than grape
What can someone do once word is gone?

Nothing-everything they do will go wrong
God reigns, He is so awesome
His Love for mankind no one can fathom
Truth and righteousness from the beginning
Reliability immense with Him you'll always win
His ways are Just He is so incredible
Help you live an abundant life on earth He's the only one capable

Account ability

Banking after dealing with family issues
Banking after wiping tears with the tissues
Receive training at home
So the nasty world can be as soft as foam
Go out into the world when you are not ready
You're on a course that's rocky and un-steady
Food dished in front you
Doesn't have to be eaten till you're full
For later some can be reserved
An action that can relate to money when earned
So when money is made it's not immediately burned
Living with parents you have your own room
There's laziness in a hoover pick up a broom
Maintain cleanliness in the confines of where you slumber
A healthy approach to learn for when you are older
Your management of the minute
Will exercise your judgement to a level acute
Learn to manage your tiny living space
Then you will have foundation for managing a larger place
Ability to initially live is learned from our parents
Ability to die is picked up from ignorance and dis-obedience
Account for your ability to live in a room with a dirty floor
Dis-obedience to your parents has brought about your flaw
A clean environment is an ability you can account for
Whether from a rich background or poor
Make the most of the small you possess
So when bigger things arrive you may have success

To laziness may I not be susceptible
By application of knowledge I live as a clean individual
May my health never remaining mediocre
My ability to stay clean not by my joints but by God's power

My faith in You a surety
Only You can account for my ability to stay clean and healthy

Aeroplanos

French *aéroplane*, from *aéro- 'air'* + Greek *-planos 'wandering.'*

Steady transiting
For a trans-Atlantic viewing
Many hours in flight
Air land and sea all in one sight
Carried thousands of miles next to a wing
Warmth of your peace making me want to sing
Referring to aeroplane wing I am not
But Heavenly Father's bosom in Your presence
By Your grace I reached new land
Eyes closed my direction orchestrated by your hand

Beginning to end you are decisive
From batter of eyelids Judgement incisive
Then comes blinking of Your eye
Before blink situations in my face mount up high
While blinked you move real swift
Entering my trouble you give me a lift
Your one blink is of similar time to me sleeping
Or could be equivalent to me breathing
Whatever the case
The Lord handles all depending on His face
His face being what He see's
What He see's being His mercies
His mercies being His lovely
His lovely being they who obey
Obey what you seem to question
The Lord's word in every section
Truth is The Love of life
The Lord loved Job, Job's sons missed out
Abraham understood without needing to shout

Shout at his sons he did
So as to reveal some of what God once hid
Obedient to God's word Job was
Only listened without awaiting a because
Acting always on the behalf of his child
Revelation of God to them was very mild
Once Job's children left to their own devise
In their lives many situations would arise
What will they do once Job is gone?
Minimal judgement differentiation between right and wrong
Job assisted sons without instruction
With Job gone absence of assistance an obstruction
All sacrifices performed in advance
Repent of own sin, Job's son had not a chance
Abraham's instruction flowed onto his servant
Confines of his room servant can personally repent
Abraham's instruction travailed through his household
Abraham's understanding of The Lord continually flowed
From brother to sister, cousin to wife
Abraham understood the truth all his life

Obedience can be likened to operation of a robot
Following instruction with feelings you have not
Then comes obedience with the answer to why
Answer being an understanding of God who reigns on High
Obedience minus understanding equals deprivation
Understanding plus obedience equals a faithful, fruitful nation

AIM

Admit Invest Mature

Admit your mistake
Why do you want to live as a fake?
It is onto your benefit
When you do wrong get your lips to admit
From top of our head to sole of our feet
From thoughts of the mind to our flesh of meat

Let the correction be invested in you
So you may help those with a pride problem too
Investment is set to grow
Mingling with evil you could make investment come slow
There's a lot to invest in your self
From wisdom to lack of sense
Confidence in actions or Mr sit on the fence
Blessings from creation and all that makes sense
Not every investment is of good health
Some can bankrupt your soul or generate you with wealth
Depending on your choice your left in one of two fields
Field of maturity or where folly yields
Folly bears no good fruit at all
Folly is like biting a cricket ball
Maturity kicks in quick and sharp
Knowing to bite an apple and string a harp
In maturity there's no room for ignorance
Steadfast in ways and walking with resilience
Maturity accounts for every action
Not wanting to receive a sanction
One day you shall become mature
Don't allow distractions to be your flaw

All Is Due

Onto You O'God all praise is due
None other in all the earth can do what You do
You alone reign on high
Name above every name from below to above the sky
As a boy with the teachers sat in the temple
People amazed, looking on You as incredible
As they rightly should
Speaking with Your understanding, at that age, no one else could
Right next to Our Heavenly Father where You are sat
Diligent obedience to a Father. You can claim that
Innocently beaten with no back chat
Cruelly whipped with punishment exact
Stayed silent when innocently accused
Clearly above suspicion while Pharisees amused
Remained wholesome and true to Your word
Pharisees walked in their talk, benignly absurd
Mistaken for being soft when You're stern
Just like money you got souls to earn, not burn
Adorned in Glory
After coming to earth and completing mission earnestly

Eyes of blazing fire
On standby, ready to fulfill God's every desire
Mingled with the sick in the head
While healing the sick on the bed
Calm as a whistle when the storms arose
Tempted by devil-Righteous ways were all You chose
Perfect example, no one can take Your stead
Angels ready to help, Your body still bled
Endured all manners of temptation to the end
Fully equipped with wisdom one can never comprehend
Thank God for being there for me
When I felt loss and in need of company

Alpha-bet

Adonai You are, people adore You
In all Your goodness I stop to
Behold; behold You in all Your beauty
Child of God I'm commissioned to be
Dead to sin, devil has no hold over me
Evil is eliminated, earth is evolving
Far be it I shall faint
Fearing Him Is first before being a formal saint
Grace from God is a gift so gentle and true
Humbling the haughty humiliating the fool
Intelligent non-intrusive and indefinite are His statutes
Jealously in our turning away so He rebukes
Keeper of Knowledge the key to eternal life
Loving kindnesses, in Him you live edification not strife
Matrimonial Messiah many marvel at Your mouth
Neutralizing the earth east to west north to south
Omnipresent omnipotent obedient King
Prayer prevails and praise is in Your dwelling
Questions arrive and You may choose to remain quiet
Reality of Our Righteous Lord is evident
Salvation of your soul is sweet and far from sour
Trials and Tribulations arise will you endure till the last Hour?
Understand His word so secrets can be unveiled
Velocity in voluntary ignorance gets you killed
Where is wisdom when you are feeling weary
Lord is not xenophobic He sees through you better than an x-ray
Youth waste time each year under impression they're young
Zero is the zeal for greatness in they that do wrong

As I am

As Un deserving as I am
First name beginning with Sam
A since birth
My whole body constructed from dust of the earth
Body partially paralysed
Keratoconus in both my eyes
A condition where shape of my eye is affected
Eye ball like rugby ball, light that enters is refracted
So every image I see is a blur
Many times I have mistaken a he for her
Picked up banana for a phone call
Kicked the floor instead of a ball

Praise shouldn't be limited
To good health or if in you joy is lifted
The moment you let your praise be conditional
Is the same moment you become partial
Partial in your praise partial in your prayer
A partiality that leaves you none the healthier
Onto God what will you render?
You have a tongue and knowledge of the alphabet
An understanding of words and how to manipulate
Construct a word or create a sentence
If not of praise then of repentance
Your heart beats within
Beats in joy or conviction of sin

On your journey from A to B
You have know how of A to Z
There's no excuse for not thanking God
In joy or sorrow
His name many shall forever hallow

Ask yourself?

Why wear trousers with no underwear?
Why go to church if immediately afterwards you curse and swear?
Why call on Jesus when trouble comes your way?
Your 23 years old, why when in danger is the only time you
decide to pray?
Did you find it amusing, stripping that boy and beating him silly?
In this action do you know that you made the devil in you happy?
I guess you want the devil to reward you with something bad?
Don't you know that's how things operate?
Do good for God He rewards you with something Good
Do Bad for devil he rewards you with sinful food
Do you know what sinful food results in?
A continuous life where all you do and think about is wrong

Would you like to know how to get out of the sinful life?
Simply walk around every day with a knife,
Actually, knife is too blunt a word to describe this wonderful tool
I'll give you a hint, it's rectangular and we used to read it in school?
Another hint, it's sharper than any double edged sword?
Yes, that's right it's the truth and knowledge
Shows you all the tricks of the devils trade
How to break the bond he may have on you as his slave
Turn away from your evil nature

Bad day good day

Sat an exam today in which I failed
My train of happiness has just been derailed
I see a man, no; I see a figure of a man
Trying to open my eyes don't think I can
He's shining too much for me to make out any features
I can feel peace coming through my whole body,
I've been made speechless
A minute ago I wanted to swear and curse
A minute ago it felt like my anger was about to burst
I failed my exam and I felt so down
I was about to shed some tears while kneeling on the ground
I'm in total shock at what is taking place
There are no tears or signs of anger on my face
A feeling
No. I'm dreaming
No. I've been drinking
Ye…No. ok. I'm Hallucinating
Yeah that's the reason….No. I've been smoking
No.
No one on earth can bring about physical reasoning
As to what it is I am truly experiencing
Because this feeling is Highly overwhelming
Never knew things existed that where so enticing
Hang on a just a minute.
I know why this is happening coming to think about it
I asked for help in my misery
Within an instant a cure came to me
Regardless of any set back
He will put you back on track
Regardless of any bad news

He will heal your pain better than ice to a bruise
When you're feeling that amplified amount of sorrow
He will fill the hurt areas that feel hollow
He who?
That person is you

Boredom And Laziness Linked BALL

To weary by dullness
Disinclination to work
A bond or a tie

Proverbs 10:26
Like vinegar to the teeth and smoke to the eyes,
So is the lazy one to those who send him.

Where do you stand?
Why for so long do you choose to sleep?
Playful is your mind and idle is your hand
What is your plan for earning your keep?
You stand at home expecting work to be done for you
Inactivity weakens the brain introducing dullness
Bedroom needs cleaning which you won't do
Unwilling to clean your body resulting in illness
To vacuum the house you find it boring
Soon as the plug is on you start yawning
Boredom of hard work
A channel for laziness to lurk
Where is boredom when you are having fun?
Laziness in pleasure of the flesh there is none
Parents are around only for so long
If you think you can always depend on them your wrong
When living alone who will clean the dishes?
One can not rely on the hubby or the misses
Preparation of a home cooked on the stove
Or washing of the dirty clothes
On your hands alone can you rely
To work on your behalf and help you get by
Working nine to five for some can be a bore
Not paying for a bill will be whose flaw?

Laziness will make small work seem a lot
Boredom may suggest you try an inept slot
Success don't like lazy it approves of diligence
To grow in life one needs to work with intelligence
Weak minds tend to travel a lot easier
Than the brain of a hard worker
Lazy hands cook little preferring take away
The diligent cook for the night during the day
What do you want to be stamped?
Lazy, with boredom as your champ
Or diligent with a busy hand
So when labour arrives you will work and not idly stand
Sleep long and work little if you will
It is your brain cells that you begin to kill
Once dead they will never grow back
Restrict your mind to games it is you that will lack
Everyone's gain is common sense and knowledge
So to procrastination we will pay little homage
Success and riches are non-bias to the normal or the lame
They with lazy hands their inheritance is not the same
The little they have will be taken
That's what happens when hard work is forsaken
What do you want to play?
Being ahead of your game
Or bowing your head in shame

Birthday

It's your birthday give off a cheer
God has blessed you with another year
No need to shed a tear
For without His grace
You wouldn't see this anniversary before your face
Your eye lids, once again, has been lifted
How will you show appreciation in the coming months?

Back On Receiving End BORE

Planted in Christ upon acceptance of salvation
Building up oneself to possibly assist the nation
Daily intake of The Word
Keeping in mind God even knows the status of the birds
Lilies are finely clothed but they don't labour or spin
Every pain is known from above your ankle to below your shin
The creator is one not to turn your back on
Your own wisdom won't last very long
Considering it is a place you have never been
A place where only God has seen
The place where only God resides
His name has dominion above and below the skies
Carnal joy in the world really bringing you death
Friends are there in riches but in trouble there is none left
Your own wisdom not enough to get you out of trouble
Turn your back on the receiving end
So you may receive the blessing God has to send
Out of God given talents what have you bore
Don't permit cowardice to be your flaw
Take care in considering life to be boring

Jesus in the garden prayed until He was sweating blood
B.O. turned RED but he wasn't Bored

Boredom

Boredom not based on my activity
Activity not based on my boredom
A minute of my life boring, I seldom
Revelation from the creator can bring on a spasm
Mystery's being revealed beyond measure
Jewellery or wisdom, which is your treasure?
Not that you can measure a mystery
If you could it wouldn't be so easy
As to why it has the name it does
Breaking into a mystery may give some people a buzz
A buzz of healthy attribute
One that can leave you whistling better than a flute
So when can one feel bored?
There is so much to meditate on
Then there's much to think of with regard to living
From the work place you enter to the place you're found sleeping
What is there to eat or what should I wear
Ignore the poor treatment or curse and swear
Read a constructive book or aimlessly watch TV
Engage in the complicated or settle for the easy
Breathe through your mouth or your nostril
Exercise your mind or leave it to evolve into a fossil
Numerous decisions to make pertaining to life
Eat dessert with a spoon or fork and knife
Do you work for the urgency to eat?
Or you just want shoes surrounding your feet
Ignorance being someone's derision
Only implies a life of lack and emptiness is their decision

Chicken

My favourite colour is green
What do you mean?
I like to eat chicken
Especially that of which is cooked in my own kitchen
If it is cooked in an area not seen
The cooks could make food even when it is not clean
When in a restaurant careful how you address those who serve you
They may mix rat droppings with your stew
The heart loves exercise
So why don't you ease off TV and rest your eyes
The body dislikes being dormant
Your spirit battles with your flesh when it comes rising from bed
Soul is malnourished when it is not fed
Need to take in the wisdom and knowledge it is our daily bread
Once soul is fed enough
It will be made strong and tough
Then when flesh battles with spirit over food for the soul
Soul will seek spiritual growth as its goal
Give your baby soul bread in small quantity
Then increase its dosage daily
Once your spirit is full and wisdom dwells in you
There is no limit to what you will do
But if you allow the good spirit to part from thee
Your body will be host to many a unproductive wayward party

Colour-fool

Blue orange or Purple
Which is the colour of a turtle?
Black white or brown
Which is the colour of the nose of a clown?
What would you like to do tomorrow?
The sea last time I saw it was yellow
I don't even remember what I did yesterday
In my mind everything seems grey
I need help it's a struggle to pray
Vision blurred I see dusty clay
Can I have some tips on how to praise?
I'm tired of living this arid phase
Open my eyes let me acknowledge your splendor
I want to know of you in advance

Relieve me of my blindness
Show me how to see and appreciate your goodness
Your goodness that fills many a mountain to the brim
Your heavy goodness that can never go slim
Craft me into a writing module
So I may note your greatness in times of trouble
Permit me an artistic hand
Thank you for the body and clothes I left the house with
Thank you for this food, you always have much to give
Thank you for my employer that awaits my arrival
Thank you for the opportunity to make that green
So I may bless those whose lives may not be serene

Condition

Upset with situation
Coping with unpleasant condition
Heart at steady pace
Tear droops streaming down my face
Anger within bursting in a tear
Heart rate is racing my vision not too clear
Wise preparation on earth is essential
Any chances afterward may not be substantial
Never been afterward to know how to proceed forward
The one who is in the after
Is the only one that knows the path to the latter
He is the only one that dwells there
Essential is accumulation of knowledge and wisdom
Assets that cannot be lost or stolen at random
Cars, houses and big TV's can be stolen or destroyed
Wisdom is eager to rest in your heart and mind
Once received, understood and applied
Will remain forever, where no thief can find

On your travels are many distractions to help you lose sight
Instant is your blindness for giving in without a fight
What is your condition?
Sit down, wail and accept current situation
Or get up, move and head in a productive direction

Here's something people know yet think of seldom
Availability of an item does not make it accessible at random

Corn

Corn on a cob
Cooked in a pan on the hob
It is the meal from yesterday
Today's Tuesday, hang on this was made on Saturday
This shirt feels really itchy
Quite a few stains sounds like shirt is screaming 'wash me!'
These blue jeans are feeling kind of tight
Its the same jeans I've worn the past fortnight
Got black shoes on my right foot
On my left I'm wearing a brown boot
Black hat shielding my scalp, which contains many a patch
Wind just blew hat in a gutter, I give up reaching for the catch
Walking alone
Can't find my way home
Walking slowly, and there's no one around
Holes in footwear, can feel surface of the ground
I like taking walks in the rain
It's how I wash my clothes, I do it over and over again
It rains weekly, down in this area
As weeks go by beard gets hairier
I've not cut my hair for at least a year
This improvised hair wash feels very good
People driving past probably wandering why I'm not wearing my
yellow hood
The yellow hood sown onto my black jacket
Bought it from pound store, but sown on label Hackett
Rain stopped touching me maybe because I'm under a bridge
I can see and hear water dripping off a ledge
Here I am, I've found my house
Directly under the bridge, think I'm sleeping next to a mouse
At every new home I have a pet

When I move into a place, it's a different one I get
I move house at least twice a week
New in this town, have no friends to whom I may speak
Under this bridge it's very cold
There's a lot of noise, nearby busy road
About to sleep, I'll use my jacket as a pillow
About to sleep, not until I eat stale bread to fill my stomach oh so hollow

D.I.Y.

Decision is yours whether you live in abundance or feel like hell
Doing it yourself, this approach to things will fare you well
Wisdom on earth is the DIY tool
DIY without knowledge can make you look a fool
Petition to the creator for tools you are in need of
So you'll be prepared like a baker wearing an oven glove
Work tools are available for your use
With everything provided can you exert an excuse?
No, none at all
Anything you say is because you answered laziness' call
Now you refuse contents of flask and lunchbox
Now you want to work at night like a fox
You have quit your day job
During the day you think of the bank you desire to rob
Go ahead and Do It Yourself
Commit your evil activities to receive quick wealth
See how far you will reach
Enemy will suck you dry worse than a leech
Once you have been used
Inside out you've been abused
You are of no use to anyone
Branded a fool and known as the devil's son
In such a situation you have absolutely no hope
Let us see how without wisdom you will cope

Hard of Hearing

Hard of hearing
Soft of listening
Intent on reading
Content in net surfing
Make noise at a funeral
But silent when asked to read for wisdom
Toaster coming down with a Heat rash
While a bank has never held cash
Kettle that is allergic to water
A lion enjoying snowy weather
Highly unhealthy is excessive pleasure of the flesh
It can leave one in a great mess
Once you get in its hard to pull out
Once you're in, wisdom and laziness engage in a bout
Moment you get a taste
Each additional encounter will lead to waste
Wages of ignorance leads to premature death
Seek wisdom now
Brothers call out to Him so He'll make you feel whole
Sisters call on Him He will fill that Hole
Stop relying on the opposite or same gender
There is none like Him
He alone can strengthen you not two hours at the gym
Let not the world use you like the 2000 swine
If you love wisdom, claim it as yours, call it mine

How I am

On 6th April 1985 I was born breach
Round to the south of my mum's body my arms did not reach
Legs came out first
Not even born yet and someone tried to curse
At the age what could I have possible done
Couldn't have offended anyone I was only my mum's son
When I was the age of three
I was asleep when something horrible happened to me
I was ever so young
I didn't understand what went wrong
I woke up to realise I was paralysed
Body was stiff could only move my eyes
Had a stroke in the right side of my brain
This caused my left side severe pain
Right side of the brain controls left side of body and vice versa
I was crying out loud for my baby sitter
I was seriously injured
Should have died but my soul still lingered
After six months in St. Mary's hospital
The doctor's and nurses were very helpful
My mum then sent me to Ghana
For 18 months I stayed with my Grandma

Someone wanted me dead
They would have preferred if I didn't wake from the bed
Whoever it was must be annoyed I'm doing too well
On my body they tried to cast a spell
Which will have no effect, not while I got the most powerful
weapon
A tool I get to use at my discretion
The use of this weapon is very simple

Before I go into detail, I'll give you the name, it's wisdom
The one to put ignorance and laziness to shame
A stroke at that age I should not be alive
Give God all the praise for letting me survive
God is mighty and extremely powerful
He kept me alive He knew I had potential
For this I am extremely grateful
I'm also honoured that I'm a vessel He can flow through

We can say words to heal and cure
Assist us to not to be mean
But keep our tongues clean
All is possible in He who strengthens me
For we control our flesh, to it we are not its slave

How it is

I woke up this morning to my sheer delight
Another day another battle to fight
It's a war deciding whether to do something wrong or right
With wisdom I've got 100% vision
Doing well is my only decision

I wasted time a lot in the past
I was on a train to Nowhere, it was going very fast
Eventually my actions slowed the train down
When it stopped I was in a totally different town
I was hesitant to let my feet touch the ground
Was very shocked at what I found
No longer in darkness I had a look around
My ears were at peace I heard not one scary sound
I saw green land, the bright sun and children at play
Thank the heavens for providing me with these eyes so I may see
Giving me these legs to walk
A mouth and voice to talk
I smile as I am thankful
Clapping my hands as a token I'm grateful

Human Torch

Feels good being a human torch
Even when I set myself alight on a wooden porch
Or if I was laying on hay
I can set my self alight and see another day
As strange as it may seem
I have many believers on my team
Set ourselves alight in different locations
We all use different motions
Doesn't matter about the time we set ourselves alight
Could be during the day or at night
Keep it burning how ever long we desire
Could be one minute or longer than an hour

A seed needs water as well as heat to grow
Acquiring wisdom provides the fire
Application of wisdom is the water flow
The person is the subject and the seed
You are responsible for what you hear and see
So, will you set yourself alight?
Or give in when wisdom and folly engage in a fight
Aimless thoughts and activity
Contributes wholeheartedly to negativity
What is your joy where is your delight
Keep your fire burning, lest you lose sight

Intense Game

Many long nights and tired mornings
Wake up drowsy 10 minutes non stop yawning
I knew after 2 hours I should have stopped playing the game
Mind is one difficult muscle to tame
Console game being new is not an excuse
Flesh is in control, Soul running around loose
If you had to read would you do so for as many hours
Read for ten minutes and you're already tired
Yet play game for ten minutes you're just getting started

Me with God and you with God is a different story
We are not carnal
But celestial beings in a physical shell
Flesh may use soul as servant

Spirit may use soul as a vessel
A time where soul and flesh may go through some trouble

Banking your body with great health
Prescribing mind with understanding of prior knowledge
Which game do you want to play?
Evil on the screen or the laziness at bay?
With one game you have the option to start over
But the other contains one life, to which will you surrender?

Left, what's right

I give up now there's nothing left
I don't know which way is right
I eat the right food making sure there is none left
I'm in the majority I do most things with my right
Leonardo di Vinci was right in the head
He would use his left hand after waking from bed
After a long dream he would paint a picture
It wasn't something small it would take longer than an hour
What he did was right
In his coffin he still manages to please people's sight
What lovely artwork he has left
Happiness in life is right ahead

A builder asked his manager what is left to do
After laying a whole foundation with super glue
Manager roared "does that look right to you?!"
"You've used the wrong substance,
What's the matter with you? Where's your sense?"
"Do you mean the common one?"
"Where's your glue I want you to drink what's left,
So you will know it's not right to deprive a brick of its cement"

Whatever one you use to right
May the other not get left behind
In amount of energy you have left
I hope you use it right

Mum

Her hand ever at the ready
Precise and remaining steady
If not letting off iron steam
Putting you to bed before laying down to dream
Injury at school after picking up that stone
Comfort of that wound once you arrive home
Emptied stomach on way to domain
Feeling woozy not much oxygen to the brain
Who has all these concerns covered?
Who about your well-being is thoughtfully bothered?

Give your mum a hand for she gives you many things with her pair

Not Gay

In the night in my room He leaves me moaning
In the morning I give Him a quickie before I'm yawning
I'm bent over during each session
Eyes closed I continue till I start sweating
He's my knight in shining armour
No one can please me better than He
When I feel His warmth inside me its overwhelming
I've never come across anything ever so calming
How about I give you a description
Of the one that brings me total satisfaction
He can be spelt with 6 letters or 9
6 letters makes you wise
9 letters keeps you in the know
The wise you can listen to or see with your eyes
The know keeps healthy and gives skin a nice glow
One is called wisdom
The other is called knowledge
Seek either to abstain from poverty

He doesn't mind if you're male or female
From when you search Him out He will treat you very well
Ever since He came inside me
My life has been good, and I feel very happy
Would you like to accept Him in your life?
He will cater to you better than any husband or wife
Call on His name, the creator of earth
Call on Him with all your heart and your breath
I hope you didn't think I was gay
That's how the ignorant like to play
Take a look at all those people in prison

They are obviously in there for a reason
They praised their ignorance by committing a crime
Ignorance pays by giving them stuff to do in their time
Laziness likes everything stank and adores all things grimy
One at a time

Runner jumps hurdle then confronts the next
Does he look at previous hurdle he flopped, he might get vexed
Then his anger will see him through the rest of the race
There's no joy in him you can tell by the look on his face
He has been so bothered about what happened in the past
Now his worries has caused him to come last
Be content with what you have ahead of you
Now this runner is going to be embarrassed at athletics school
Worrying is procrastinations subtle but harmful device
Solidifying your thoughts quicker than ice
Let go of your past burdens and worries
At least now you can tell your children some true stories

Wisdom is available to improve on yesterday, no time for sorrow
Use time wisely to excel today, not yesterday or tomorrow

Fretting about yesterday or worrying about next day will leave
productivity hollow
One action at a time
Success is progressive, many a step before you reach your prime
Every action has a reaction
Each man in control of their misery or satisfaction
Action in completing daily task
Will cause reaction of success, abundance and more

Pay Day

When you go to work it is you that will get paid
Don't worry about your colleague and how he behaved
You are what you eat
Have to work to put shoes on your feet
You are where you live
Blessed with a job now you must learn to give
A new frame of mind you should seek to engage
Your income about to increase to a new range
Need wisdom on how to handle such a huge amount
Fingers won't be enough to help you count
Were you blessed with a job so you can keep money to yourself?
Or so you can share some of your wealth
On your income you're highly content
Food, clothes and some change after the rent
An offer from another job that pays more
Salary too good to be true there is no flaw
What do you do?
Wrong choice could lead to your contempt
Make a decision that you won't later resent
Not every pay is of monetary value
Money is of value, psychic income is too
Motive for being on time your reason for arriving late
You know there's a pay bracket for your inactivity
The wage is a path toward poverty, that payment is heavy
You bring it on yourself
If you forget to seek more wisdom after you gained wealth
I got no time for sympathy
Depending on whom you hang around they may show some empathy
Tithe and offering
That's according to your faith-as for me I won't mention
Turn to what is good denounce your lazy way
Otherwise you will have hell on earth to pay

Range

Everyday people wake up it's like another page
Some go through happiness some go through rage
Range
Some people in the world always have something to eat
Other people barely have vitamins, or on their body any meat
Range
Majority of houses clean and tidy
Some homes are messy, vile and unhealthy
Range
Some people don't eat meat and are vegetarian
Those some people can add up to make nation
Range
Some people are living on earth like it's heaven
Each person has option it is their decision
Some will spend their lives as though living in hell
All because they followed ignorance and followed it's ruthless spell
Range
Some believe in God and all things nice
While some can't sleep until they have done a bank heist
Range
There are they that are dark in skin
And there are those that are dark within
Range
Just because you have loads of Uni degrees
Or you are surrounded by money up to above your knees
It does not make you hot
Lawyers use aftershave and get paid very well
Street cleaners get paid just enough and their clothes often smell
Range
Birds fly in the sky
Leopards walk around eating, their brain can't think why?
Courtrooms have humans in them because they can talk

They have humans in them because creation gave humans sense
and the ability to walk
Humans can think (well some), and animals can't
People can sing and some animals chant
Range
Some trees produce fruit
Other trees just look bold and cute
Range
You didn't come out your mother the size you are
At the age of two you wouldn't be able to throw a tennis ball very far
When you were born you were smaller than you are now
You are growing and people see it as wow

People perish for lack of Knowledge
Some prefer procrastination's ledge
Range
Stranger pours hot coffee on his shirt
His face frowns immediately he must be hurt
Uttering many foul words he sounds very angry
Understandable, incident taken place at a party
Be angry and do not transgress in any way
A range of emotions flying through your body
Body responds to the words you say
Give it instruction, it will obey

Right and left hemisphere

1% read and write
Seems small for all the information we recite
5% total usage
Many don't even reach this stage
95% where memory is held
Barely gets a visit, like a rapist in jail
Left hemisphere deals with science and math, grammar and words
Qualities needed to recognise and describe something absurd
Right Hemisphere deals with science of philosophy and intonation
Reliable quality for distinguishing accents from any nation
Then there is the backbone of all interaction with the brain
The spine controls all messages including those relating to joy
or pain
Brain needs blood to receive its oxygen and nutrients
Brain needs blood so it can supply body it's supplements

Lack of knowledge is no excuse
Keep your body in check the foolish let theirs run loose
Good or evil, you got a brain to distinguish
One you must cling to, the second you should relinquish
Cells die upon in-activity
Your brain is vast, a huge facility
May as well use it to its full potential
So your ways are not menial or substantial
There is no reason don't permit the ignorance
Use left hemisphere to form words of repentance
Engage right hemisphere to identify the evil
Use memory to follow wisdom as your sample
Giving God praise by either reading or writing
Live today for you know not if you'll wake in the morning

Society

How's life growing up in this society
Eye witness account unsure turns out to be apparently
Neck hurts as I walk down the street
Constantly having to stare at my feet
If I see people as I walk
They grip tight their belongings and seize to talk
Getting on a bus can be such a nightmare
Passengers clutching belongings and continuing to stare
Then comes the hassle of making an income legally
No one will hire yet I have a GCSE
They say I need experience
How will I get experience if they won't give me a chance?
The rat race music plays on but I refuse to dance
Will I be useful in a riot
Or productive as a pilot?
How will I earn a living?
I'm pre-judged as one that deals in robbery and killing
Unemployment appears to be the only solution
Question?
What kind of person do you think you are seeing?
It's me, just like you, a Human being

Square Root

May I be square rooted no more
Shape me like item used by a foot to score
Mould me into a wholesome vessel
Mould me in preparation for my days of trouble
Smash out my bad points
Put to work my idle joints
Smooth out my bent path
In my trials teach me to laugh
Permit me to cut no more corners
The moon is round its air impure
Crooked people in the world
Yet spherical is the earth's core

Before being born many have failed
Born into various twists and turns
A little bit of work some complain it burns
Some reach teenage years
Mingling with smoke and drinking beers
The straight path they endeavour to ignore
Bent way they'll walk to their definite fall
Only so much can be said
Speak all you like, some are eager to be dead
Stay on your straight and narrow
Give in to none lest you receive immediate sorrow
Some are so crooked
They can sway you because you looked
It is in your best interest to stay in line with wisdom heard
Any other route you're bound to look absurd

Stress

How many words have you spoken?
You want it closed it stays open
You want it open it stays closed
Could be talking about memory could be talking about clothes
You hold it open to express
Keep it closed to suppress
You do one to conceive
You do the other to relieve
Right now I'm referring to stress
Which affects your manner and the way you dress
Speak your mind and exert all worries
Free your head think of happy stories
Take a seat, have something to drink
I mean water, not alcohol, if that's what you think

Think Warm

Keep me company
In your absence I feel lonely
I want just one minute with thee
Your brother hastens my need to pee
He gives me a shiver
The leaves in his presence begin to wither
He's so cold and bitter
His breath freezes water
He's impartial whether it's autumn or winter
My knight in shining armour
My warmth equivalent to the heat of the sun's mid hour
Come and comfort me
No more deprivation
My love for you, I've made my declaration
Why the absence?
I yearn for your essence
If you had an account I would transfer many a pence

My body is tense I'm trying to keep warm
I need a little heat, some shelter from this storm
This isn't like you, far from the norm
Are we in the same country
Or are you far away
My eyes tightly closed I'm picturing our last encounter
Such beauty, blissful joy, innocent banter
Rolling in the grass, no care for time or whatever
These thoughts have warmed me up a little
Oh no, it wasn't my thoughts
You're here, yes, you're here
My muscles have relaxed
My breathing is calm
My breathe is now untaxed

I needn't use lip balm
How comes you ended up coming?
Not that I'm complaining
It'd be great to know a reason
So next time there'll be no fretting

Is that a serious answer
Don't toy with my feelings I need something good and proper
You're telling me
Let me repeat for clarity
That my thoughts of you made you arrive
The more I thought about being cold
Or why you weren't here by my side
These thoughts made me less bold
This is the first time I have thought in a long time
Since then my mind has been playing back old memories
Or worrying about things that are a mental disease
Coming to think about it I've not thought for the majority of life
Playback of past experiences
Or future projection of unlikely instances

40 percent of the things I worry about will never happen
30 percent of things over and past that can't be changed by all the
worry in the land of the living
Needless worries about my health rakes in at 12 percent
10 percent on petty, miscellaneous worries equaling time
poorly spent
Real, legitimate worries 8 percent
Less than a tenth of the French cent
Only 8 percent of my worries are worth concerning myself about
92% percent are pure fog with no substance or clout
The thought with the lowest percentage
Has the highest advantage

I guess it's true what they say
Whatever I think about
I bring about
On any given day
With children words count

Working with children in a food store
They're supposed to be adults I can't take no more
Serving adults, children are my colleagues
Workers range from 20 to late thirties
Supposed to be grown but so immature
They got education, but common sense is their flaw
Different newspapers have different reading age
Some papers have more pictures than words per page
Reading which shows you are at a higher stage
Pictures convey a message from joy to rage
People in gallery analyse picture with intense greed
Encrypting message accurately with speed
Anyone can read words written on a wall
As for a picture, it's not easy for all
Changed your mind on which paper to read?
FT, no pictures just words, economic brain you need
To paint picture with words you see
Thought it was best constructing words from picture in gallery
Who said they are not the same
Specialise in both so you're in the game
Read so you may construct a picture so lovely
Analyse pictures so you can create a beautiful story
How about pictures in a magazine
The one showing celebrities that want to be seen
What story could you create from that?
I mean a picture with a bridge, heavy rain and a cat
Your brain is there to be filled
Lack of knowledge in life gets you killed
Teachers all over are willing to teach
Just have to go to them, will you reach?

Parents just there to give birth to you?
WRONG!
Parents just here to make rice and stew
WRONG!
Parents are there to nurture you
Feeding sub-conscious with wisdom invaluable
Obedience to their ways you'll find easier to commit
Whether directly
Or indirectly
All qualities you learnt from your parents
Make your peace if you once disliked them or their presence
Plead your forgiveness sink deeper than low
Attitude to parents is how you'll treat future partner or didn't you know?

You what?

Associate why with regret
When it comes to when people sometimes forget
Why ask why when what is more significant
Don't need to know why if you are un-available
Or do you?

The relevant of irrelevance
Could cost you more time than earning 5 pound 20 pence
What is it you expect?
Be joyful you're within the Who
Better than being in bad broth or hideous brew
Careful what counsel you seek- could be a fake
What do you do to be in with the Who?
Settle your mind on seeking wisdom, there's your clue
Where do you go to get the What you asked for?
Not the same place for girls, drinks and all
Highly informed on one yet misinformed on the other
Informed on the corrupted and sadly informed on something grater
The where could be a building
Or outdoors, wherever you're comfortable to do some thinking

Love your neighbour as yourself
Loving your neighbour shall generate in you great health
You are responsible for your body and its operation
If you don't work you don't eat
Who do you expect to put shoes on your feet?
Why pray for things that your hands can fix
Deal with things your hands were made to handle
Ignorance gets you nowhere except a heap of trouble
Why pray train to arrive at your destination
When you can research the time train will arrive at the station
It is a waste of time that you don't have to waste
Can counter being late by waking up with haste

About the Author

A gentleman with a rich personality. Born in London 1985, roots born and bread in Ghana, west Africa. A Masters graduate with over 10 years teaching and mentoring experience. Car enthusiast and active listener. A poet with a passion to enrich the lives of others.

w: www.samuelappiah.co.uk
m: samuel@samuelappiah.co.uk

Printed in Great Britain
by Amazon